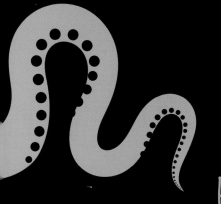

PAIGE TOWLER

 FOREWORD BY SY MONTGOMERY

Author of the *New York Times* best seller
The Soul of an Octopus

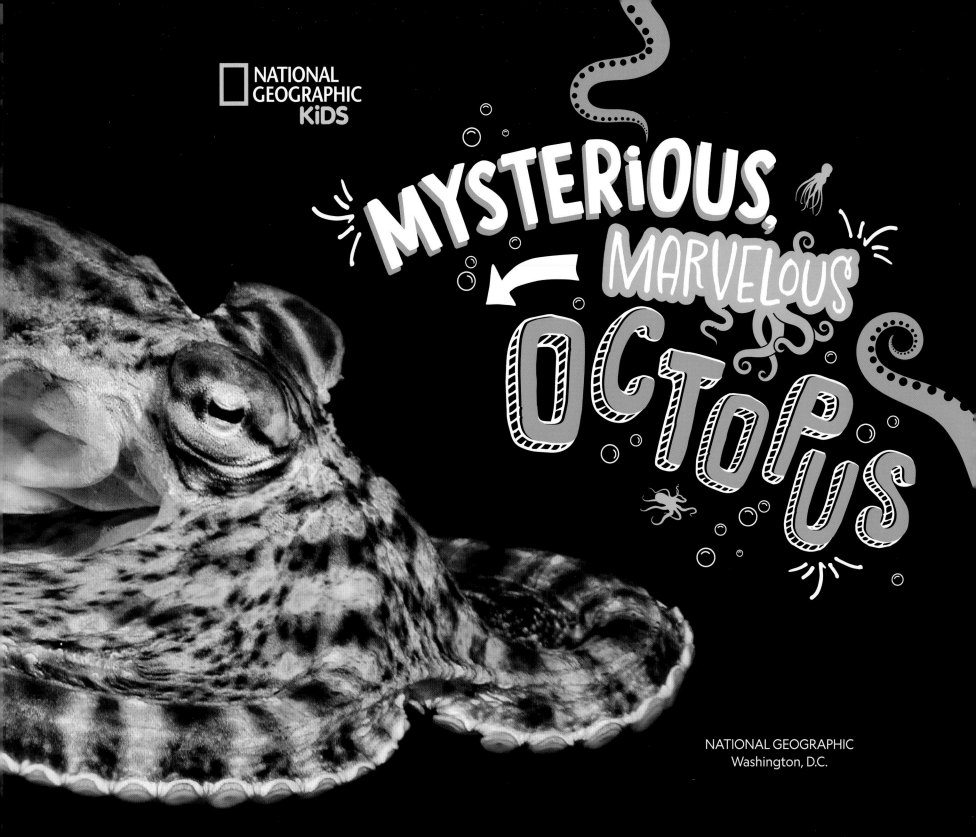

NATIONAL GEOGRAPHIC
KiDS

MYSTERIOUS, MARVELOUS OCTOPUS

NATIONAL GEOGRAPHIC
Washington, D.C.

FOREWORD

Think of it: What if you could change color and shape? What if you had not just 10 fingers, but 2,000 of them? Now imagine you could squeeze your whole body through an opening the size of an orange. And on top of that, you could taste with your skin, squirt ink, and jet through the sea by squirting water out of a funnel in the side of your head!

Sounds like some comic book superhero, or a made-up space alien in a story. But these powers are real, and they belong to a creature living right here on our planet with us—one with eight arms, blue blood, and three hearts: the octopus.

There are actually hundreds of different kinds of octopuses living all over the world's seas. Some can grow to hundreds of pounds. Some are so small they would fit on your finger. (And speaking of fingers, the 2,000 the octopus has aren't really fingers. They're better! Instead of 10 fingers on two hands, they have more than 200 suction cups on the inside of each arm. Each one is able to fold and bend so well that an octopus can even untie a knot in a slender thread.)

In the pictures and words ahead, you're about to meet one of the smartest and coolest creatures on planet Earth. And not only do these squishy sea creatures have superpowers we humans can only dream of; octopuses are also really smart.

They solve puzzles. They learn quickly. They especially love squeezing through mazes, and remember the twists and turns they took to do it even faster next time.

Octopuses also like to have fun. In public aquariums, like ones you may have visited, keepers give the octopuses toys to play with. They enjoy LEGO bricks. They take apart, and sometimes put together, Mr. Potato Head. They play with some of the same toys you probably like to play with.

So prepare to make friends with an octopus. Get ready to shake hands—times eight!

Your friend,

Sy Montgomery
Author of *Inky's Amazing Escape, The Octopus Scientists, The Soul of an Octopus,* and *Secrets of the Octopus*

Across the **SLOSHING, SALTY BRINE**

awaits a **TREASURE** tough to find.

It isn't **coin**, or **gold**, or **gem**—

It's **FAR** more

MARVELOUS

than them.

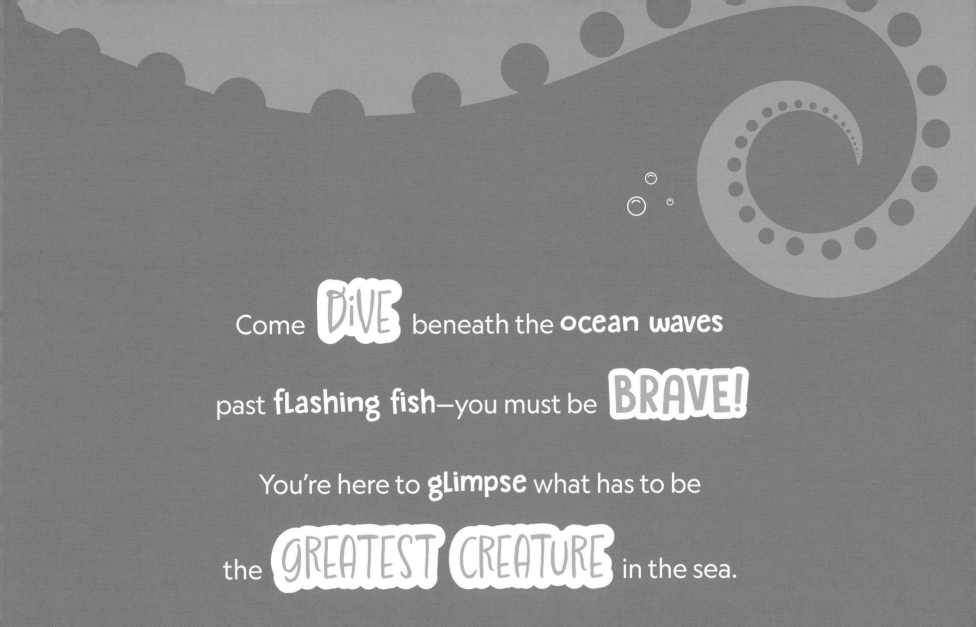

Come **DIVE** beneath the **ocean waves**

past **flashing fish**—you must be **BRAVE!**

You're here to **glimpse** what has to be

the **GREATEST CREATURE** in the sea.

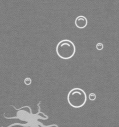

It has **EIGHT ARMS!**
And **suckers,** too!

It's **tough to spot,** but when you do:

You see that it was **worth the fuss**

TO INTRODUCE ...

🐙 MEET THE OCTOPUS

Say hello to one of the most magical creatures in the ocean! You can spot an octopus by its soft body and eight arms. Octopuses live in ocean waters around the world. They can be found everywhere from warm, shallow seas to deep, dark, chilly waters.

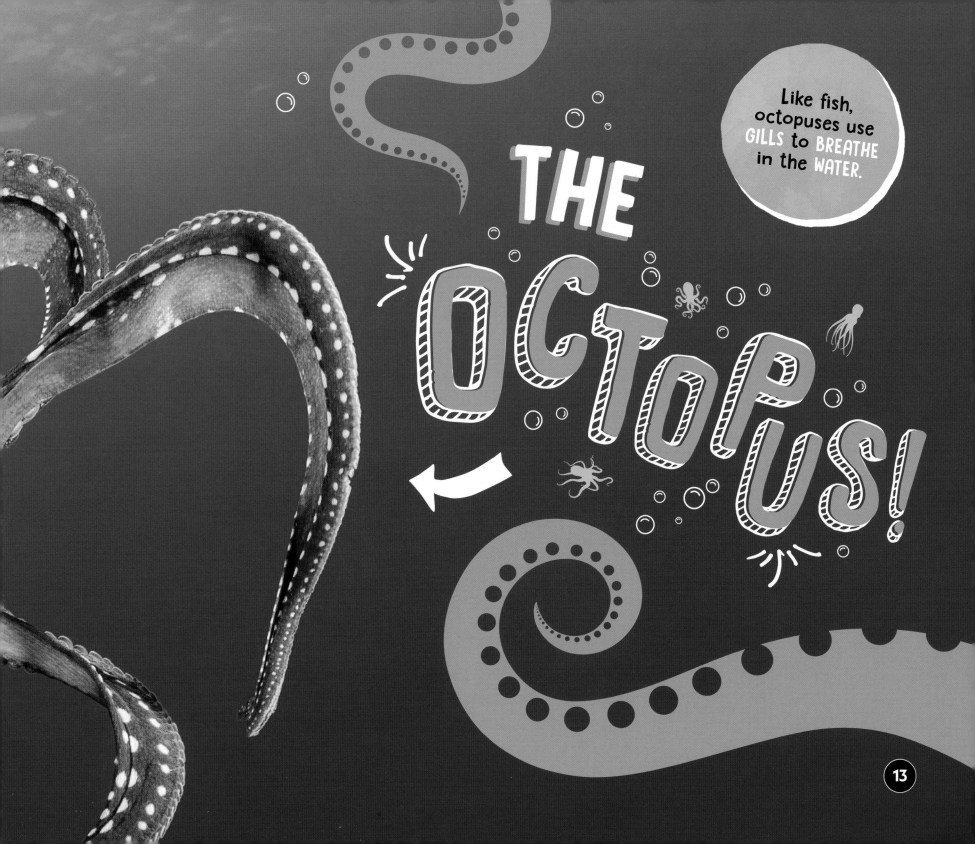

THE OCTOPUS!

Like fish, octopuses use GILLS to BREATHE in the WATER.

13

OH, TELL ME:

Have you ever GLIMPSED

a thing MYSTERIOUS as this?

GOING SOLO

What makes an octopus so mysterious? For one thing, octopuses can be hard to find. They are usually nocturnal. This means that they are most active at night. These shy creatures also spend lots of time hiding, whether under rocks or in reefs. On top of that, most octopuses live alone. They might sometimes meet up with another octopus, but most of the time, octopuses hang out by themselves. They prefer their own company!

Whether its size is **HUGE** or **SMALL,**

this **cryptic creature** has it all:

a **HIDDEN BEAK** to dine on prey ...

SUPER SIZES

Octopuses come in many different sizes. Some, like the giant Pacific octopus, can be enormous. They can grow as long as a giraffe is tall. Others, like the argonaut, are much smaller. They can be shorter than your pinkie finger!

DINNERTIME

Octopuses usually eat small ocean animals like crabs, shrimps, and lobsters. Octopuses often hunt their prey by sneaking up on it. They then use their strong arms to grab the prey. Each octopus arm is covered in suction cups. These suction cups, or suckers, help the octopus hold on. An octopus also uses its suckers to smell and taste its food! Then the octopus eats a meal using its beak. That's right—octopuses have a beak, just like birds!

BEAK

... **DARK INK** for making **getaways** ...

A DARING ESCAPE

Octopuses aren't the only hungry animals in the sea. Other ocean animals sometimes try to snack on octopuses. These hungry animals can include large fish, seals, and whales. Luckily, octopuses are very good at escaping danger. Octopuses have special body parts called ink glands that make a dark liquid known as ink. When an octopus feels scared, it can shoot a large cloud of ink into the water. The dark ink makes it hard to see. The octopus can quickly swim away!

BRiLLiANT BODiES

What else makes an octopus so mysterious? Its body is very different from yours! Where most humans have two arms, an octopus has eight. And instead of one heart, an octopus has three. An octopus's three hearts keep its (blue!) blood moving around its body. They also help keep its gills working. This lets the octopus breathe underwater. But that's not all. Humans have only one brain, but octopuses have nine! Each octopus has one central brain and eight other brains that are spread out in small bundles in its body. That means an octopus has brains in its arms! This lets the octopus control each arm separately from the others.

... NINE BRAINS that lend it **super smarts**,

blue blood, big eyes,

THREE BEATING HEARTS!

SENSATIONAL!

You might **applaud**

this **sublime, superb** CEPHALOPOD!

Cephalopods have **EXISTED** on Earth for more than **500 MILLION YEARS.** That means they were around before the dinosaurs.

Hold on—there's MAGIC left in store!

Just wait for its **chromatophores**

to cast a DAZZLING show of **shades**

like **purple, red,** or **Lemonade.**

CURIOUS CHROMATOPHORES

Octopuses can change colors! This is thanks to something called chromatophores (kro-MAT-uh-fors). Every living thing is made up of tiny building blocks called cells. Octopuses have special cells that are filled with different colors. These cells are called chromatophores. Octopuses use chromatophores to make themselves look many different colors. Octopuses can turn gray, pink, blue, brown, green, and more! This helps the octopus hide in plain sight. It can hide from danger. It can also surprise its prey.

WARNING SIGNS

Scientists think that all octopuses have venom. Venom is a type of toxic substance an animal uses to hunt or to defend itself. Some animals inject, or deliver, venom by stinging other animals. Others, like octopuses, deliver venom through their bites! Even though the blue-ringed octopus can be smaller than a human hand, it is the octopus known for having the strongest venom! Their venom helps these tiny octopuses hunt shrimps and crabs.

But not just **magic** ... **DANGER,** too,

lies swirling in **electric blue**

And **sparkling spots:** The sudden sight

might mean a **tingling, DEADLY BITE!**

Or else, an OCTOPUS can take

the SHAPE of jelly, crab, or snake,

or smooth stingray! Spined Lionfish!

to SNATCH a hidden fishy dish.

Mimic octopuses can COPY the SHAPES of at least 15 other ANIMALS! This one looks like a sea star!

MASTER MIMIC

Like other octopuses, the mimic octopus can change color. But this octopus has even more amazing abilities. Mimic octopuses can make themselves look like other animals! They do this by moving their bodies into different shapes. They also copy other animals' behavior. But why?

Mimic octopuses often do this to surprise their prey. When an octopus is pretending to be a fish, a real fish might not be scared of it! Mimic octopuses also change shape to scare away danger. To do this, they make themselves look like animals that can sting or bite.

🐙 OCEAN ARMOR

Octopuses have very soft bodies. This means that they need to protect themselves from other hungry animals. Luckily, octopuses are very clever. Some octopuses carry around empty shells—sometimes coconut shells or the shells of other animals. When the octopus needs to hide, it can crawl inside the shell!

And speak of HiDiNG, please don't tell,

but sometimes one might **find** a SHELL

and **haul it** on its **octo-back,**

then CRAWL iNSiDE if it's **attacked.**

OH, TELL ME,

how **could** one dismiss

a **creature** MARVELOUS as this?

In **salty waters** 'round the world:

SPOTTED, RINGED,

or STRIPED, or PEARLED,

There are about 300 KINDS of octopuses on Earth.

35

Slick octopuses **GLIDE** and **PLAY,**

and **SWIM** from **dusk** till **break of day,**

 OCTOPUS GAMES

Just like people, octopuses have different personalities and moods. An octopus might feel shy and spend its time hiding. Or it might feel curious and move closer for a look at something it has never seen before. An octopus might even feel playful! Octopuses in zoos and aquariums have been known to play tricks on the people who work there. In the wild, some octopuses have been caught stealing crabs from fishing boats. In fact, scientists are learning more about octopus personalities all the time—and about what makes them so wonderful.

And then, when **RESTING** is in store,

CRAWL in their **dens**

and **close the door.**

DELIGHTFUL DENS

Octopuses live in homes called dens. Many octopuses make their dens in rocks. Others use materials like coconuts or shells to build their dens. When an octopus is ready to sleep, it squeezes inside its den. But does it really close the door? Yes! Some octopuses block off their dens by pulling rocks or shells over the entrance.

Oh, tell me now—who could resist

a **creature**

as **MYSTERIOUS**

and **MARVELOUS** ...

AS THIS??

OCTOPUS GALLERY

All octopuses have eight arms and a round, soft body. They can do the amazing things you've read about in this book. But different species—or types—of octopuses look different and sometimes do different things. There are hundreds of different types of octopuses. Here are the species you've seen in these pages.

California Two-Spot Octopus

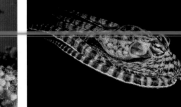
Day Octopus

Mimic Octopus

Southern Keeled Octopus

Pygmy Octopus

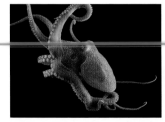
California Two-Spot Octopus

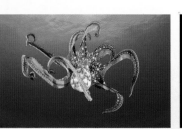
Day Octopus

Blue-Ringed Octopus

Argonaut

Giant Pacific Octopus

Caribbean Reef Octopus

Argonaut

Day Octopus

Argonaut

Common Octopus

Blue-Ringed Octopus

Deep-Sea Octopus

Giant Pacific Octopus

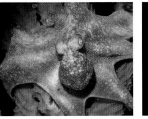
Caribbean Reef Octopus

Blue-Ringed Octopus

Mimic Octopus

Coconut Octopus

Blanket Octopus

Common Octopus

Starry Night Octopus

Blue-Ringed Octopus

Caribbean Reef Octopus

Mimic Octopus

Day Octopus

Coconut Octopus

Day Octopus

Dumbo Octopus

Caribbean Reef Octopus

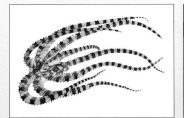
Wunderpus Octopus

Day Octopus

Caribbean Reef Octopus

Poison Ocellate Octopus

Long-Arm Octopus

Coconut Octopus

45

GLOSSARY

cell: a small, living unit that makes up all living creatures

cephalopod: a type of marine animal that has a head attached to at least eight arms

chromatophore: a cell that creates color

gill: the organ some animals use to breathe underwater

gland: an organ in a living creature that makes different substances

invertebrate: an animal with no backbone

nocturnal: being active mostly at night

prey: an animal that is caught by another for food

CREDITS

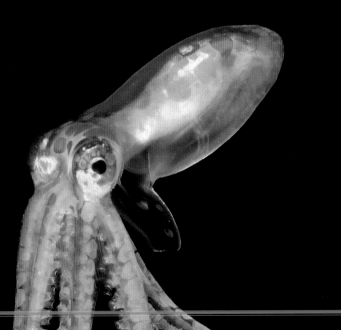
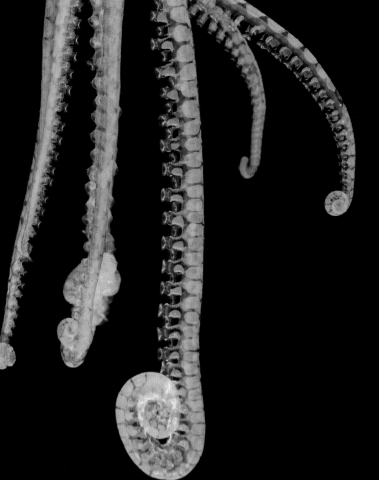

For Joel. —PT

NATIONAL GEOGRAPHIC and Yellow Border Design are trademarks of the National
Geographic Society, used under license.

Since 1888, the National Geographic Society has funded more than 14,000
research, conservation, education, and storytelling projects around the world.
National Geographic Partners distributes a portion of the funds it receives from
your purchase to National Geographic Society to support programs including the
conservation of animals and their habitats. To learn more, visit natgeo.com/info.

For more information, visit nationalgeographic.com, call 1-877-873-6846,
or write to the following address:

National Geographic Partners, LLC
1145 17th Street NW
Washington, DC 20036-4688 U.S.A.

For librarians and teachers: nationalgeographic.com/books/
librarians-and-educators

More for kids from National Geographic: natgeokids.com

For rights or permissions inquiries, please contact National Geographic Books
Subsidiary Rights: bookrights@natgeo.com

Designed by Amanda Larsen

Names: Towler, Paige, author.
Title: Mysterious, marvelous octopus / Paige Towler.
Description: Washington, D.C. : National Geographic Kids, 2024. I Audience:
     Ages 5-8 I Audience: Grades 2-3
Identifiers: LCCN 2023007240 I ISBN 9781426376672 (hardcover) I ISBN
     9781426376825 (library binding)
Subjects: LCSH: Octopuses--Juvenile literature.
Classification: LCC QL430.3.O2 T69 2024 I DDC 594/.56--dc23/eng/20230424
LC record available at https://lccn.loc.gov/2023007240

Many thanks to the book team: Kathryn Williams, editor; Lori Epstein,
photo director; Sarah Gardner, photo editor; Alix Inchausti, production editor;
and Lauren Sciortino and David Marvin, associate designers.

Printed in China
23/HHC/1